What's the Weather?

IT'S HAILING!

By Alex Appleby

Gareth Stevens
Publishing

Please visit our website, www.garethstevens.com. For a free color catalog of all our high-quality books, call toll free 1-800-542-2595 or fax 1-877-542-2596.

Library of Congress Cataloging-in-Publication Data

Appleby, Alex.
It's hailing! / by Alex Appleby.
  p. cm. — (What's the weather)
Includes index.
ISBN 978-1-4339-9393-0 (pbk.)
ISBN 978-1-4339-9394-7 (6-pack)
ISBN 978-1-4339-9392-3 (library binding)
1. Hail — Juvenile literature. 2. Weather — Juvenile literature. I. Appleby, Alex. II. Title.
QC929.H15 A66 2014
551.57'87—dc23

First Edition

Published in 2014 by
Gareth Stevens Publishing
111 East 14th Street, Suite 349
New York, NY 10003

Copyright © 2014 Gareth Stevens Publishing

Editor: Ryan Nagelhout
Designer: Andrea Davison-Bartolotta

All illustration by Michael Harmon

Printed in the United States of America

CPSIA compliance information: Batch #CS13GS: For further information contact Gareth Stevens, New York, New York at 1-800-542-2595.

Contents

I play with
my friend Tim.
We play outside.

5

The sky looks dark.
It starts to hail.

The hail is big.
Each piece is
an inch wide.

They look like golf balls!

We run inside.
We wait until it stops.

Then we go outside.
We put some hail
in a red bucket.

It is cold.
It feels like ice!

Mom says it is made from layers of ice.

19

The hail melts.
It turns to water.

We use it to water
Mom's plants.